AARON JAY KERNIS

AIR

for Cello and Piano

AMP 8104

First printing: September 1996

ISBN 978-0-7935-6398-2

Associated Music Publishers, Inc.

DISTRIBUTED BY

7777 W. BLUEMOUND RD. P.O. BOX 13819 MILWAUKEE, WI 53213

PROGRAM NOTE

Air is songlike and melodic, and it is the "purest" and sparest piece I've written in a few years. It contains many hymn- or chant-like elements, and though rooted in E♭ major, it retains a kind of plaintive quality more reminiscent of minor or modal tonalities. Formally, it combines a developing variation form with a simple song form.

—AARON JAY KERNIS

duration: ca. 11 minutes

to Evelyne

AIR

Aaron Jay Kernis
1995
transcribed for cello by
Carter Brey and the composer

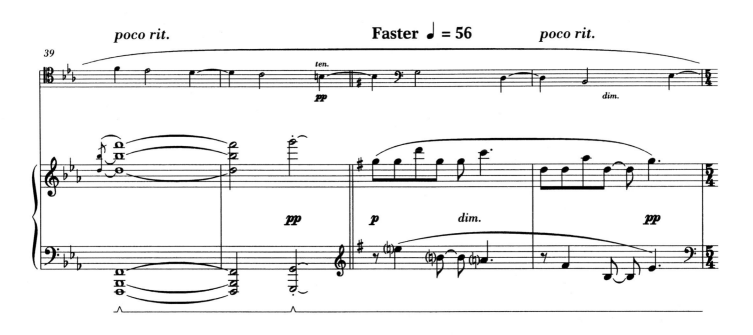

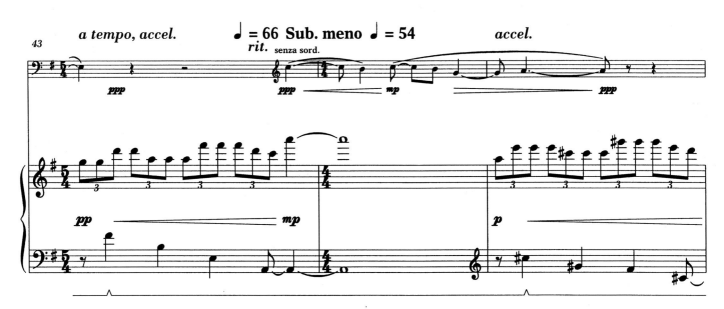

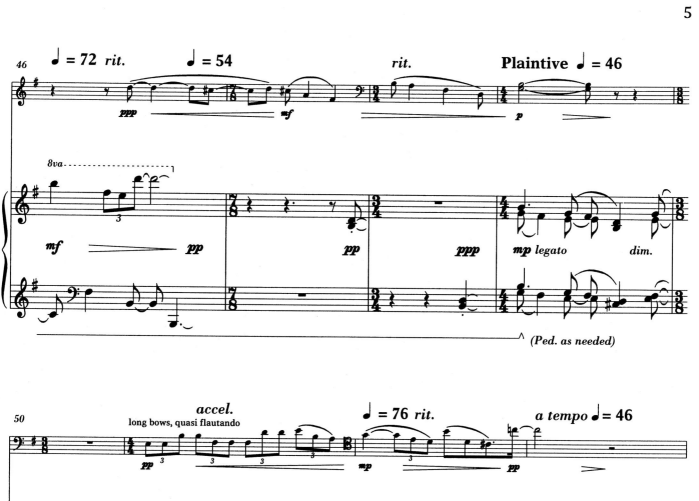

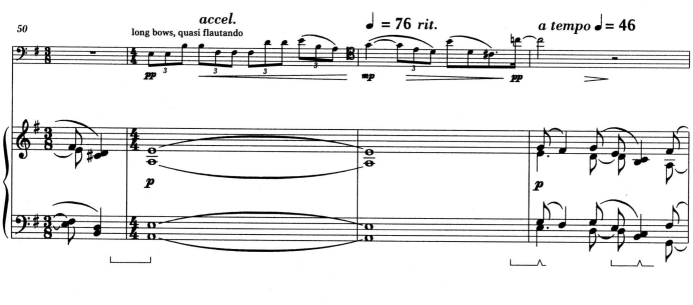

Passionate, heavy, intense ♩ = 48

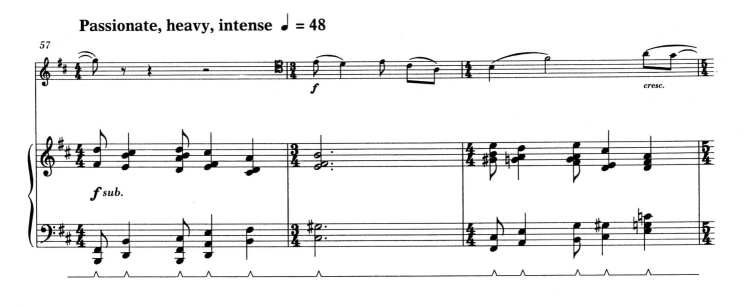

AARON JAY KERNIS

AIR

for Cello and Piano

Cello

AMP 8104

First printing: September 1996

ISBN 978-0-7935-6398-2

Associated Music Publishers, Inc.

DISTRIBUTED BY

HAL•LEONARD®

7777 W. BLUEMOUND RD. P.O. BOX 13819 MILWAUKEE, WI 53213

AIR

Aaron Jay Kernis
1995

transcribed for cello by
Carter Brey and the composer

Cello

Gentle, singing, plaintive ♩ = 46 – 50

Cello

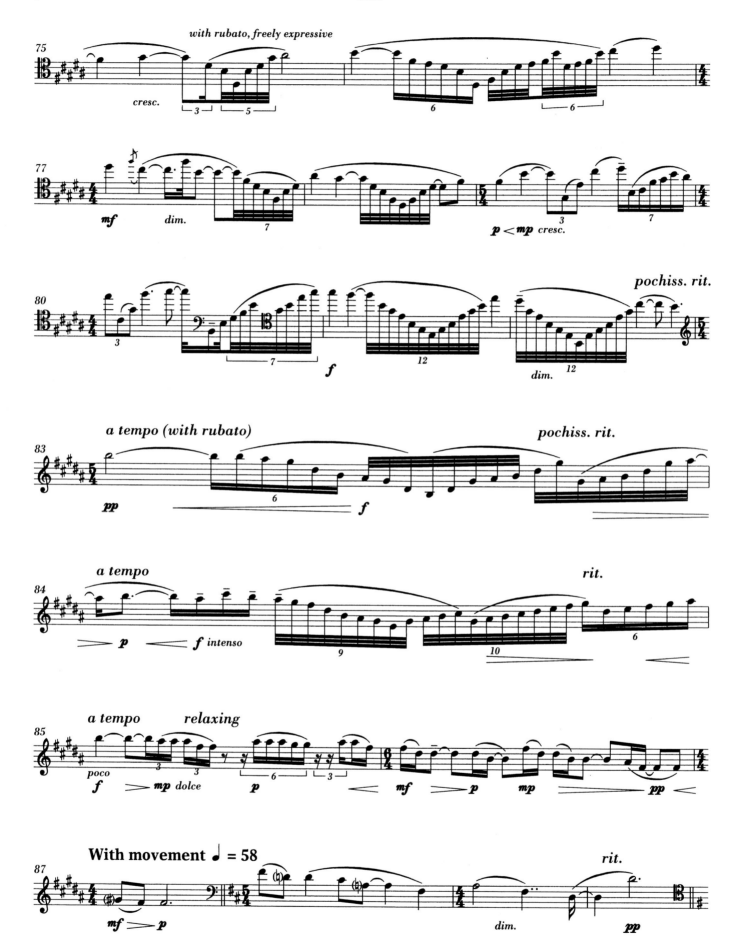

Più adagio ♩ = 42

senza rit.

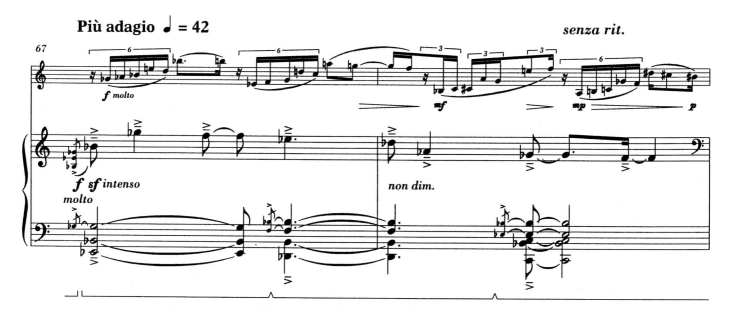

Tranquil ♩ = 44 – 48

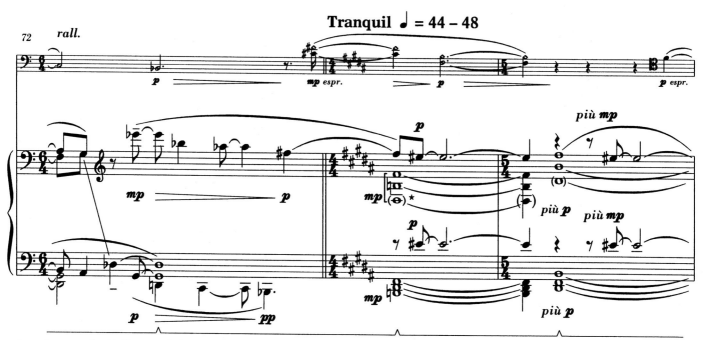

* omit notes in ( ) if stretch is too large.

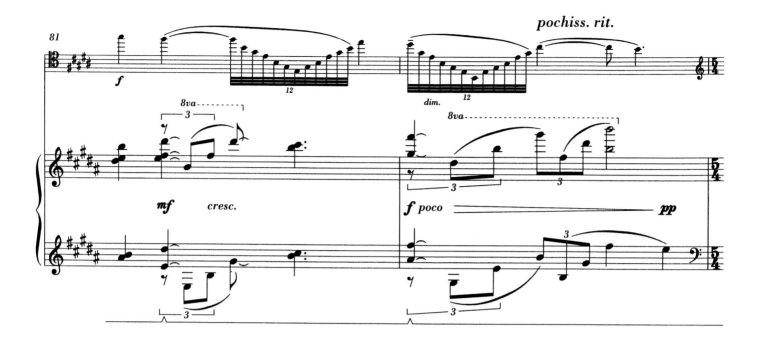

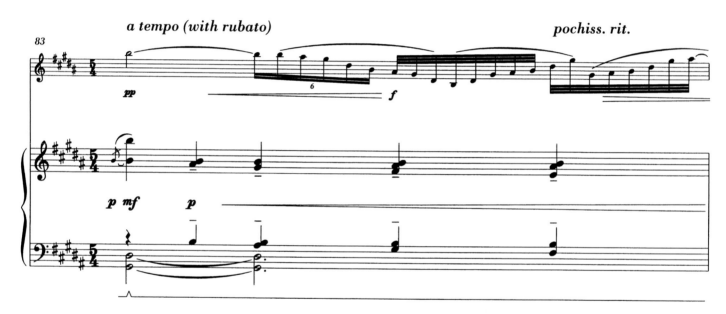

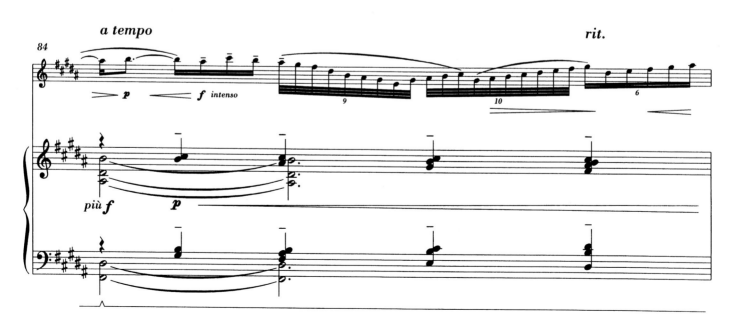

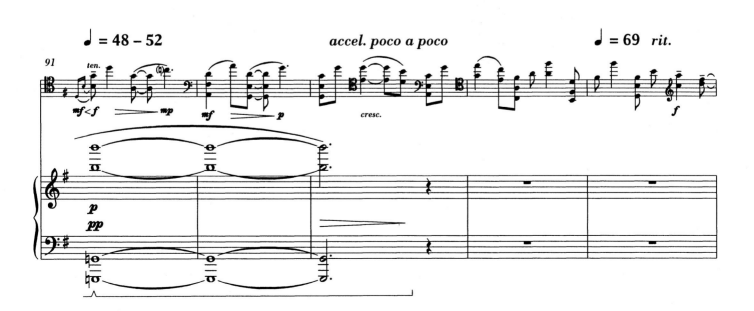

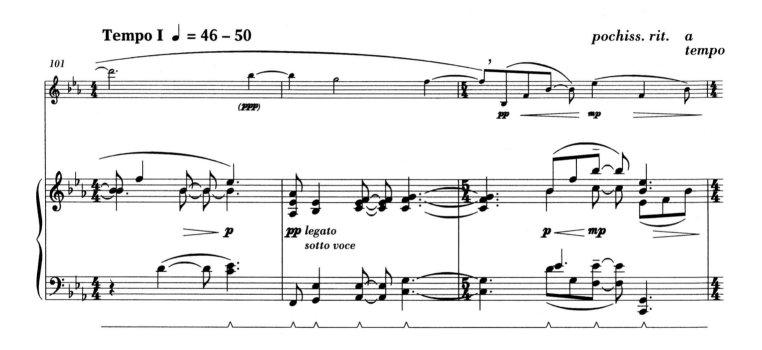